John Kember and Marguerite Wilkinson

Violin Sight-Reading 2

Déchiffrage pour le violon 2
Vom-Blatt-Spiel auf der Geige 2

A fresh approach / Nouvelle approche
Eine erfrischend neue Methode

ED 12837
ISMN M-2201-2384-9
ISBN 978-1-902455-54-9

www.schott-music.com

Mainz · London · Madrid · New York · Paris · Prague · Tokyo · Toronto
© 2007 SCHOTT MUSIC Ltd, London · Printed in Germany

ED 12837

British Library Cataloguing-in-Publication Data.
A catalogue record for this book is available from the British Library
ISMN M-2201-2384-9
ISBN 978-1-902455-54-9

French translation: Agnès Ausseur
German translation: Uta Pastowski
Design by adamhaystudio.com
Music setting and page layout by Jackie Leigh
Printed in Germany S&Co.8043

Contents
Sommaire/Inhalt

4

Preface

Violin Sight-Reading 2 aims to build on the sight-reading skills learnt in book 1 and provides a wealth of more challenging examples so that the pupil may gain even greater confidence when approaching any new piece of music for the first time.

There are five sections in this publication, each of which gradually introduces new notes, rhythms, articulations, keys, Italian terms and musical styles in a logical sequence, much as you would find in a violin tutor. The emphasis is on providing idiomatic tunes and structures rather than sterile sight-reading exercises.

Each section begins with several solo examples and concludes with duets and accompanied pieces, enabling the player to gain experience of sight-reading within the context of ensemble playing.

The reader is urged to consider each piece for its rhythmic content from the outset, but with awareness of tempo and style. Students are encouraged to perform each piece in the manner of the style indicated, and to play not only fluently but also musically and expressively: an interesting and musically-shaped performance is always preferable to one that is technically correct but dull.

Section 1 revises the keys and time signatures covered in book 1. It also includes both simple and compound time and positional shifts.

Section 2 introduces the keys of E♭ and A♭ major, and 1st- to 2nd-position shifts of both a tone and a semitone.

Section 3 introduces the keys of C minor and F minor and extends the range to include top D and E. Further dotted rhythms are used together with some syncopations and chromatic movement.

Section 4 extends to keys of D♭ major and B major. The time signatures of 5/4, 5/8 and 7/8 are encountered. Ornaments are introduced and other tonalities, including atonal examples.

Section 5 explores various tonalities, including modal and chromatic, together with time and key changes within a piece. An extensive range of notes and styles are given.

To the pupil

The objective of these pieces is to encourage the habit of sight-reading, both in solo form and in duets and accompanied pieces, in order to help you prepare for reading in solo and ensemble situations.

Rhythm should be your first consideration and a pulse should be established in your mind before you begin to play. Musical style and mood can be established by observing the tempo and expression marks.

Be constantly aware of the key and accidentals required in each piece and look out for changes which may occur in both the accidentals and the time signatures.

Above all, aim to **play musically** by creating shape as indicated by the dynamics, articulation and phrasing. Call on your experience to give a stylistic, expressive and musical interpretation at all times.

Knowledge and fluency of the scales and arpeggios for the keys used in this book will always help your technical facility when it comes to the fingering patterns encountered throughout each piece.

Reading at sight is an essential 'life' skill for musicians. It will give you the **independence** to explore **your choice** of music for yourself, drawing from either material from the past or from today's popular repertoire.

> **Always** take care to observe time, key signatures and accidentals
> **Always** make accuracy of rhythm a priority
> **Always** aim to maintain continuity and pulse
> **Always** attempt to play musically

Be independent: be free to choose, explore, and enjoy!

5

Préface

Déchiffrage pour le violon 2 s'appuie sur les aptitudes de lecture à vue acquises dans le volume 1 et présente une foison de configurations plus exigeantes qui renforceront l'assurance de l'élève lors de sa première approche d'une pièce de musique.

Les cinq parties de ce volume introduisent progressivement notes, rythmes, articulations, tonalités, termes italiens et style musicaux nouveaux selon un ordre logique respectant celui d'une méthode de violon. Le propos est ici d'offrir des morceaux de musique et des structures caractéristiques du jeu violonistique de préférence à de stériles exercices de déchiffrage.

Chaque partie débute par plusieurs morceaux en solo et se referme sur des duos et des pièces accompagnées qui familiariseront le violoniste avec le déchiffrage collectif.

Le lecteur est fortement incité à envisager en priorité le contenu rythmique de chaque pièce, tout en considérant le *tempo* et le style, et à interpréter chaque pièce dans le style indiqué avec aisance, musicalité et expression. Une interprétation construite et musicale sera toujours préférable à une exécution techniquement correcte mais sans relief.

La section 1 Révision des tonalités et mesures rencontrées dans le volume 1 ; mesures simples et composées et changements de positions.

La section 2 Introduction des tonalités de *mi*♭ majeur et de *la*♭ majeur ; déplacement d'un ton et d'un demi-ton avec changement de la 1ère position à la 2ème position.

La section 3 Introduction des tonalités de *do* mineur et de *fa* mineur et extension de la tessiture au *ré* et *mi* aigus ; rythmes pointés, syncopes et mouvements chromatiques.

La section 4 Extension des tonalités jusqu'à *ré*♭ majeur et *si* majeur ; introduction des mesures à 5/4, 5/8 et à 7/8 ; introduction des ornements et de l'atonalité.

La section 5 Tonalités diverses, échelles modales et chromatiques et changements de mesure et de tonalité en cours de morceau ; large étendue de notes et de styles.

A l'élève

L'objectif des pièces contenues dans ce volume est d'encourager chez vous l'habitude du déchiffrage en solo, en duo et avec accompagnement, de manière à vous familiariser avec la lecture à vue en soliste ou dans un ensemble.

Le rythme doit constituer votre première préoccupation et vous devrez établir mentalement une pulsation avant d'attaquer. Le style musical et le climat du morceau découleront de l'observation des indications de *tempo* et de nuances.

Ayez constamment la tonalité de chaque pièce et les altérations qu'elle comporte présentes à l'esprit. Repérez les changements d'altérations et de mesure.

Avant tout, jouez **avec musicalité** en respectant le caractère défini par les nuances dynamiques, les articulations et le phrasé. Faites appel à votre propre expérience pour donner à tout moment une interprétation musicale, stylée et expressive.

La connaissance et la maîtrise des gammes et arpèges des tonalités utilisées dans ce volume avantageront votre aisance technique dans les enchaînements des doigtés des motifs rencontrés dans chacun des morceaux.

La lecture à vue est une pratique de « survie » essentielle à tout musicien. Elle procure l'**indépendance** permettant l'exploration personnelle de la musique de **votre choix**, tirée du répertoire connu, passé ou actuel.

Toujours, observer les indications de mesure, de tonalité et les altérations
Toujours considérer l'exactitude rythmique une priorité
Toujours maintenir la continuité et la pulsation
Toujours s'efforcer de jouer avec musicalité

L'indépendance, c'est la liberté de choisir, d'explorer et de se faire plaisir !

Vorwort

Vom-Blatt-Spiel auf der Geige 2 möchte auf den in Band 1 erlernten Fähigkeiten des Vom-Blatt-Spiels aufbauen und bietet eine Menge anspruchsvoller Beispiele. Auf diese Art und Weise kann man mehr Vertrauen gewinnen, wenn man neue Musikstücke zum ersten Mal spielt.

Der vorliegende Band besteht aus fünf Teilen, in denen nach und nach neue Noten, Rhythmen, Artikulationen, Tonarten, italienische Begriffe und Musikstile in einer logischen Abfolge eingeführt werden, ganz ähnlich wie in einer Geigenschule. Der Schwerpunkt liegt mehr auf der Bereitstellung passender Melodien und Strukturen als auf abstrakten Vom-Blatt-Lese-Übungen.

In jedem Teil findet man zuerst einige Solobeispiele und anschließend Duette und begleitete Stücke, damit man auch beim Zusammenspiel mit anderen Erfahrungen im Vom-Blatt-Spiel sammeln kann.

Bei jedem Stück sollte von Anfang an auf den Rhythmus geachtet werden, allerdings immer unter Berücksichtigung des Tempos und des Stils. Die Schüler sollen dazu ermutigt werden, jedes Stück in dem angegebenen Stil zu interpretieren. Dabei sollte aber nicht nur flüssig gespielt werden, sondern auch musikalisch und ausdrucksvoll. Eine interessante und musikalisch gestaltete Darbietung ist immer einer technisch korrekten, aber ausdruckslosen Darbietung vorzuziehen.

Teil 1 wiederholt die Tonarten und Taktarten, die in Band 1 enthalten sind. Man findet außerdem einfache und zusammengesetzte Takte sowie Lagenwechsel.

Teil 2 führt die Tonarten Es-Dur und As-Dur ein sowie Lagenwechsel von der 1. Lage in die 2. Lage in Ganzton- und Halbtonschritten.

Teil 3 führt die Tonarten c-Moll und f-Moll ein, und der Tonumfang wird durch das hohe D und das hohe E erweitert. Außerdem werden punktierte Rhythmen sowie synkopische und chromatische Bewegungen verwendet.

Teil 4 erweitert die Tonarten um Des-Dur und H-Dur, und es werden der 5/4-, 5/8- und der 7/8-Takt. Außerdem kommen Verzierungen und atonale Beispiele vor.

Teil 5 beschäftigt sich mit verschiedenen Tonarten, darunter auch mit modalen und chromatischen Tonarten. Außerdem kommen Takt- und Tonartwechsel mitten im Stück vor, und man findet eine große Auswahl an Noten und verschiedenen Stilen.

An den Schüler

Die vorliegenden Stücke möchten dazu beitragen, Erfahrungen im Vom-Blatt-Spiel zu sammeln, sowohl bei Solostücken als auch bei Duetten und Stücken mit Begleitung. Dadurch wird das Vom-Blatt-Spiel alleine und auch im Ensemble gefördert.

Bevor man zu spielen beginnt, sollte man als erstes den Rhythmus beachten und in Gedanken das entsprechende Tempo festlegen. Den musikalischen Stil und die Stimmung erkennt man an der Tempoangabe und der Vortragsbezeichnung.

Man sollte sich immer der Tonart und der erforderlichen Vorzeichen im Stück bewusst sein und auf Wechsel während des Stückes achten, die sowohl die Vorzeichen als auch die Tonart betreffen können.

Spiele vor allem **musikalisch** und berücksichtige beim Spielen die angegebenen dynamischen Angaben, Artikulationen und Phrasierungen. Nutze deine Erfahrung, um zu jeder Zeit eine stilistisch korrekte, ausdrucksvolle und musikalische Interpretation zu ermöglichen.

Die flüssige Beherrschung der Tonleitern und Akkorde in den Tonarten, die in diesem Band vorkommen, ist für die technische Umsetzung der in den Stücken vorkommenden Fingersätze hilfreich.

Das Vom-Blatt-Lesen gehört zu den grundlegenden Fertigkeiten, über die jeder Musiker verfügen sollte. Es ermöglicht eine gewisse **Unabhängigkeit**, das Stück selbst auszuwählen und zu entdecken, sowohl Werke aus der Vergangenheit als auch heute gängiges Repertoire.

> Achte **immer** auf die Taktart, Tonart und Vorzeichen
> Der genaue Rhythmus hat **immer** oberste Priorität
> Das Tempo sollte **immer** kontinuierlich beibehalten werden
> Versuche **immer** musikalisch zu spielen

Versuche es einfach: selbst auswählen, ausprobieren, Neues entdecken – und habe einfach Spaß beim Musizieren!

Section 1 – Revision
Section 1 – Révision
Teil 1 – Wiederholung

Reading at sight: giving a musical performance

1. Look at the **time signature** and check for any changes of time within the piece. Tap the rhythm, feeling the pulse throughout. Count at least one bar in your head before you begin to play.

2. Look at the **key signature**. Identify which notes sharps and flats apply to. Also look for **accidentals** in the piece and work out fingerings.

3. Look for **patterns**. While tapping the rhythm, look at the melodic shape and notice movement by step, skip, repeated notes and sequences.

4. Observe the **articulations** and **dynamics**.

5. Make a **musical performance** of each piece. Before you begin to play, observe the character of the music given in the performance directions. Look ahead while playing, and keep going.

La lecture à vue est une exécution musicale

1. Vérifiez l'**indication de mesure**. Repérez tout changement survenant au cours du morceau. Frappez le rythme en maintenant une pulsation intérieure constante. Comptez au moins une mesure mentalement avant d'attaquer.

2. Vérifiez l'**armure de la tonalité**. Repérez à quelles notes s'appliquent les dièses et les bémols. Recherchez également les **altérations accidentelles** et établissez les doigtés.

3. Repérez les **motifs**. Tout en frappant le rythme, observez les contours mélodiques et les déplacements par degré, les sauts d'intervalles, les notes répétées et les séquences.

4. Examinez les **phrasés** et les nuances dynamiques.

5. Donnez une **interprétation musicale** de chaque pièce. Avant d'attaquer, cernez le caractère de la musique à l'aide des indications d'exécution. Lisez à l'avance pendant que vous jouez et ne vous arrêtez pas.

Vom-Blatt-Spiel: Die musikalische Darbietung

1. Schaue dir die **Taktangabe** an und prüfe, ob im Stück irgendwelche Taktwechsel vorkommen. Schlage den Rhythmus, wobei du immer das Metrum spüren solltest. Zähle mindestens einen Takt im Kopf vor, bevor du zu spielen beginnst.

2. Achte auf die **Tonartvorzeichen** und finde heraus, zu welchen Noten die Kreuz- und B-Vorzeichen gehören. Suche auch nach weiteren **Vorzeichen** im Stück und erarbeite entsprechende Fingersätze.

3. Achte auch auf die **Muster**. Schaue dir die melodische Form an, während du den Rhythmus schlägst, und achte auf Bewegungen in Schritten oder Sprüngen, sich wiederholende Noten und Sequenzen.

4. Beachte die **Artikulationsbezeichnungen** und **dynamischen Angaben**.

5. Jedes Stück sollte wie eine **musikalische Darbietung** gespielt werden. Bevor du zu spielen beginnst, solltest du den Charakter des Stückes beachten, der in der Vortragsbezeichnung angegeben ist. Sei beim Spielen vorausschauend und spiele immer weiter.

Performance directions used in this section:

Alla marcia	in a march style
Allegretto	not as fast as allegro
Allegro	fast, quick and lively
Allegro molto	very fast
Andante	at walking pace
Con moto	with movement
Dolce	sweetly
Energetico	energetically
Espressivo	expressively
Giocoso	joyfully
Grazioso	gracefully
Legato	smoothly
Mesto	sadly
Minuetto	a short, stately piece in 3-time
Moderato	at a moderate tempo
Ritmico	rhythmically
Sostenuto	sustained
Spiritoso	with spirit, animated
Vigoroso	vigorously
Vivace	lively
Vivo	lively, briskly

Indications d'exécution utilisées dans cette section :

Alla marcia	en style de marche
Allegretto	modérément rapide
Allegro	rapide
Allegro molto	très rapide
Andante	allant
Con moto	avec mouvement
Dolce	doux
Energetico	énergique
Espressivo	expressif
Giocoso	joyeux
Grazioso	gracieux
Legato	lié
Mesto	triste
Minuetto	menuet – courte et majestueuse danse à trois temps
Moderato	modéré
Ritmico	rythmique
Sostenuto	soutenu
Spiritoso	spirituel
Vigoroso	vigoureux
Vivace	vif
Vivo	vif, animé

Vortragsangaben für Teil 1:

Alla marcia	marschmäßig
Allegretto	weniger bewegt als Allegro
Allegro	schnell, lebhaft und heiter
Allegro molto	sehr schnell
Andante	gehend
Con moto	mit Bewegung
Dolce	süß
Energetico	energisch
Espressivo	ausdrucksvoll
Giocoso	fröhlich
Grazioso	anmutig
Legato	gebunden
Mesto	traurig
Minuetto	kurzes, majestätisches Stück im 3/4-Takt
Moderato	in gemäßigtem Tempo
Ritmico	rhythmisch
Sostenuto	verhalten, getragen
Spiritoso	geistreich, lebhaft
Vigoroso	energisch, kräftig
Vivace	lebhaft
Vivo	lebhaft, flott

Section 1 – Revision
Section 1 – Révision
Teil 1 – Wiederholung

1.

2.

3.

Alla marcia

4.

Spiritoso

5.

Grazioso moderato

6.

Allegretto

7.

Giocoso

8.

Sostenuto e espressivo

9.

Vivo spiritoso

10.

Andante sostenuto

11.

Andante espressivo

12.

Allegro moderato

13.

Allegretto

14.

Grazioso e espressivo

14

17.

19.

Minuetto grazioso

20.

Andante e dolce

21.

Allegro vivace

23.

Mesto e sostenuto

24.

Section 2 – Introducing the keys of E♭ and A♭ major; tone and semitone shifts

Section 2 – Introduction des tonalités de *mi♭* majeur et de *la♭* majeur ; déplacements d'un ton et d'un demi-ton

Teil 2 – Einführung der Tonarten Es-Dur und As-Dur; Lagenwechsel in Ganzton- und Halbtonschritten

Reading at sight: giving a musical performance

Identify the **character** of the piece – fast, slow, happy, march etc.

Observe the **time** and **key signatures** together with the **accidentals**, **dynamics**, **articulations** and any **other instructions**.

Choose an **appropriate speed**, both for the piece and for yourself – ensure you are going to be comfortable enough to make a musical and technically accurate performance at the first attempt. Count at least one bar before you begin to play so as to secure the right speed.

While playing, always **look ahead** so that you have time to prepare for what is coming. In addition to playing the **right notes** with **rhythmic accuracy**, keep paying attention to all of the details as they occur: slurs and tongued notes, staccato, dynamics and any other instructions in the score.

La lecture à vue est une exécution musicale

Définissez le **caractère** de la pièce : rapide, lent, joyeux, en style de marche, etc.

Repérez les indications de **mesure** et de **tonalité**, ainsi que les **altérations accidentelles**, les **nuances**, le **phrasé** et toutes **autres indications**.

Prenez un **mouvement adapté** au style de la pièce et vous convenant. Assurez-vous d'être assez à l'aise pour donner une exécution techniquement et musicalement juste dès votre première tentative. Comptez au moins une mesure avant d'attaquer afin d'installer le bon mouvement.

Lisez toujours **à l'avance** pendant que vous jouez pour vous préparer à ce qui suit. Tout en exécutant les notes avec **justesse** et **rigueur rythmique**, soyez constamment attentif à tous les détails qui se présentent : notes liées, *staccato*, nuances et toutes autres indications figurant dans la partition.

Vom-Blatt-Spiel: Die musikalische Darbietung

Bestimme den **Charakter** des Stückes – schnell, langsam, fröhlich, marschartig usw.

Beachte die **Taktart** und **Tonartvorzeichnung** sowie die **Vorzeichen, dynamischen Angaben, Artikulationsbezeichnungen** und **sonstigen Anweisungen**.

Wähle ein **angemessenes Tempo**, das sowohl zum Stück als auch zu dir selbst passt und achte darauf, dass du dich in der Lage fühlst, beim ersten Versuch eine musikalisch und technisch korrekte Darbietung zu präsentieren. Zähle mindestens einen Takt vor, bevor du zu spielen beginnst, damit du im richtigen Tempo bist.

Sei beim Spielen immer **vorausschauend**, damit du genügend Zeit hast, um das, was als nächstes kommt, vorzubereiten. Achte außer dem Spielen der **richtigen Noten** mit dem **exakten Rhythmus** darauf, dass du alle anderen Hinweise beachtest: Legatobögen, Staccato, dynamische Angaben und alle weiteren Anweisungen, die in der Partitur stehen.

Performance directions used in this section:

Adagio	very slow and expressive
Alla	in the style of
Allegretto	not as fast as Allegro
Andante	at walking pace
Andantino	slightly faster than Andante
Brillante	bright, sparkling
Cantabile	in a singing style
Con moto	with movement
Espressivo	expressively
Gavotte	a stately dance beginning at the half bar
Giocoso	playful, humorous
Grazioso	gracefully
Maestoso	majestically
Moderato	at a moderate tempo
Poco allegro	a little fast
Poco lento	a little slowly
Ritmico	rhythmically
Scherzando	playful, joking
Semplice	simply
Sostenuto	sustained
Vivace	lively
Vivo	lively, briskly

Indications d'exécution utilisées dans cette section :

Adagio	lent
Alla	à la manière de
Allegretto	moins rapide qu'*allegro*
Andante	allant
Andantino	un peu plus vite qu'*andante*
Brillante	brillant
Cantabile	chantant
Con moto	avec mouvement
Espressivo	expressif
Gavotte	danse majestueuse débutant à la moitié de la mesure
Giocoso	joyeux
Grazioso	gracieux
Maestoso	majestueusement
Moderato	modéré
Poco allegro	un peu rapide
Poco lento	un peu lent
Ritmico	rythmé
Scherzando	en badinant
Semplice	simplement
Sostenuto	soutenu
Vivace	vif
Vivo	vif, animé

Vortragsangaben für Teil 2:

Adagio	sehr langsam und ausdrucksvoll
Alla	im Stil von
Allegretto	weniger bewegt als Allegro
Andante	gehend
Andantino	etwas schneller als Andante
Brillante	glänzend
Cantabile	gesanglich
Con moto	mit Bewegung
Espressivo	ausdrucksvoll
Gavotte	ein majestätischer Tanz, der in der Regel mit einem Auftakt beginnt
Giocoso	spielerisch, humorvoll
Grazioso	anmutig
Maestoso	majestätisch
Moderato	in gemäßigtem Tempo
Poco allegro	etwas schnell
Poco lento	etwas langsam
Ritmico	rhythmisch
Scherzando	scherzhaft
Semplice	einfach
Sostenuto	zurückhaltend
Vivace	lebhaft
Vivo	lebhaft, flott

24

Section 2 – Introducing the keys of E♭ and A♭ major, tone and semitone shifts

Section 2 – Introduction des tonalités de *mi♭* majeur et de *la♭* majeur, déplacements d'un ton et d'un demi-ton

Teil 2 – Einführung der Tonarten Es-Dur und As-Dur, Lagenwechsel in Ganzton- und Halbtonschritten

25.

26.

27.

28.

Giocoso

29.

Allegretto

30.

Andante sostenuto

31.

Maestoso

26

32.

Vivace

33.

Andantino

34.

Vivo

35.

Alla gavotte

36.

Andante cantabile

37.

Allegretto

38.

Ritmico

39. **Poco allegro**

Mixolydian mode.   Mode mixolydien.   Mixolydisch.

40.

Ritmico

41.

Sostenuto e espressivo

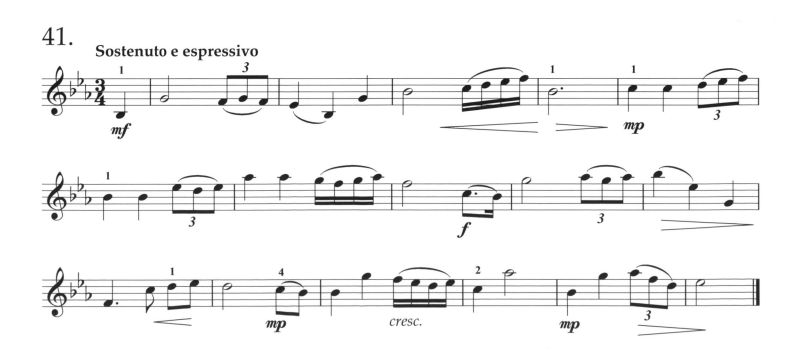

42.

45.

48.

Andante

49.

Adagio sostenuto

50.

51.

52.

Poco lento

53.

54.

55.

Section 3 – New keys of C minor and F minor
Section 3 – Nouvelles tonalités de *do* mineur et de *fa* mineur
Teil 3 – Neue Tonarten: c-Moll und f-Moll

Swing rhythms
Swing rhythms are what most people think of as 'jazz', with its easily recognisable, relaxed triplet feel. The Swing Era began in the 1940s and 1950s – the era of the Big Bands of Glenn Miller, Benny Goodman and Count Basie, and of singers Nat King Cole and Ella Fitzgerald.

Jazz quavers can be notated in two ways:

or

both played

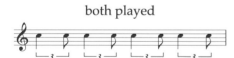

La rythmique *swing*
La rythmique *swing*, facilement reconnaissable à son allure ternaire libre, est généralement associée au jazz. L'ère du *swing* s'installa dans les décennies 1940 et 1950, époque des *Big Bands* de Glenn Miller, de Benny Goodman et de Count Basie et des chanteurs Nat King Cole et d'Ella Fitzgerald.

On note les « croches jazz » de deux façons :

ou :

toutes deux joués ainsi :

Swingrhythmen
Meistens denkt man bei Swingrhythmen an den Jazz mit seinen leicht erkennbaren lockeren Triolen. Die Ära des Swing begann in den 1940er und 1950er Jahren – in der Zeit der Big Bands von Glenn Miller, Benny Goodman und Count Basie sowie der Sänger Nat King Cole und Ella Fitzgerald.

Die Achtelnoten können im Jazz auf zwei verschiedene Art und Weise notiert werden:

oder:

Beide werden folgendermaßen gespielt:

The double sharp
Piece 84 contains the note F✗, notated:

A **single sharp** raises the note by **one** semitone.
A **double sharp** raises the note by **two** semitones.

Le double dièse
La pièce n° 84 comporte la note *fa* ✗, notée :

Le **dièse** élève la note d'**un** demi-ton.
Le **double dièse** élève la note de **deux** demi-tons.

Das Doppelkreuz
Das Stück Nr. 84 enthält die Note F mit Doppelkreuz, die wie folgt notiert wird:

Ein **einfaches Kreuz** erhöht die Note um **einen** Halbton.
Ein **Doppelkreuz** erhöht die Note um **zwei** Halbtöne.

Performance directions used in this section:

Allegretto	not as fast as allegro
Allegro	fast, quick and lively
Andante	at walking pace
Andantino	a little faster than andante
Brillante	bright, sparkling
Capriccioso	fancifully
Con moto	with movement
Deciso	decisively
Doloroso	sadly
Espress.	expressively
Grandioso	in a noble, grand style
Grazioso	gracefully
Habanera	a dance from Cuba (Havana)
Legatissimo	very smoothly
Legato	smoothly
Misterioso	mysteriously
Moderato	at a moderate tempo
Nobilmente	with nobleness
Poco lento	a little slowly
Presto	very fast
Ragtime	a dance form popular in America in the 1890s
Ritmico	rhythmically
Sempre	always (*sempre legato* – always smoothly)
Spiritoso	with spirit, animated
Vivace	lively, quick

Indications d'exécution utilisées dans cette section :

Allegretto	moins rapide qu'*allegro*
Allegro	rapide
Andante	allant
Andantino	un peu plus vite qu'*andante*
Brillante	brillant
Capriccioso	capricieux
Con moto	avec mouvement
Deciso	décidé
Doloroso	douloureux
Espress.	Expressif
Grandioso	grandiose, noble
Grazioso	gracieux
Habanera	danse originaire de Cuba
Legatissimo	très lié
Legato	lié
Misterioso	mystérieux
Moderato	modéré
Nobilmente	avec noblesse
Poco lento	un peu lent
Presto	très vite
Ragtime	forme de danse américaine des années 1890
Ritmico	rythmé
Sempre	toujours
Spiritoso	spirituel
Vivace	vif, animé

Vortragsangaben für Teil 3:

Allegretto	weniger bewegt als Allegro
Allegro	schnell, lebhaft und heiter
Andante	gehend
Andantino	etwas schneller als Andante
Brillante	glänzend
Capriccioso	launisch, phantasiereich
Con moto	mit Bewegung
Deciso	bestimmt
Doloroso	schmerzlich
Espress.	ausdrucksvoll
Grandioso	großartig
Grazioso	anmutig
Habanera	kubanischer Tanz aus Havanna
Legatissimo	sehr gebunden
Legato	gebunden
Misterioso	geheimnisvoll
Moderato	in gemäßigtem Tempo
Nobilmente	edel
Poco lento	etwas langsam
Presto	sehr schnell
Ragtime	beliebte Tanzform in Amerika in den 1890er Jahren
Ritmico	rhythmisch
Sempre	immer (*sempre legato* – immer gebunden)
Spiritoso	geistreich, lebhaft
Vivace	lebhaft

Section 3 – New keys of C minor and F minor
Section 3 – Nouvelles tonalités de *do* mineur et de *fa* mineur
Teil 3 – Neue Tonarten: c-Moll und f-Moll

56.

57.

58.

63.

Moderato

64.

Andante

65.

Deciso

69.

70.

71.

72.

Vivace e ritmico

73.

Capriccioso

79.
Ritmico

80.

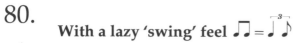

81.

82.

Habanera

83.

Andante con moto

84.

85.

Allegretto non troppo
Ragtime feel

Section 4 – Introducing D♭ major and B major; 5/4, 5/8 and 7/8 time; ornaments

Section 4 – Introduction des tonalités de *ré*♭ majeur et de *si* majeur ; mesures à 5/4, 5/8 et 7/8 ; ornements

Teil 4 – Einführung der Tonarten Des-Dur und H-Dur; Der 5/4-, 5/8- und 7/8-Takt; Verzierungen

Ornaments in music

Acciaccatura (from the Italian Acciaccàre: 'to crush').
Notated as a small quaver with a diagonal line through the stem

The acciaccatura is played quickly, 'crushed' against the next note.

Appoggiatura (from the Italian Appoggiare: 'to lean').
Notated as a small quaver, but without the diagonal line:

The appoggiatura usually takes half the value of the following note.

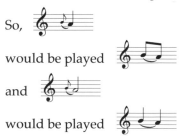

So,

would be played

and

would be played

Ornementation de la musique

Acciaccatura **(appogiature brève)**, (de l'italien *acciaccàre*, écraser).
Notée comme une petite croche dont la hampe est barrée en diagonale :

L'*acciaccatura* est jouée rapidement, « écrasée » contre la note suivante.

Appogiature (de l'italien *appoggiare*, appuyer).
Notée comme une petite croche mais sans barre diagonale :

L'appogiature dure habituellement la moitié de la valeur de la note qui la suit.

Ainsi

s'exécute

et

s'exécute

Musikalische Verzierungen

Acciaccatura (vom italienischen Wort „acciaccàre": zerdrücken, zerquetschen).
Die Acciaccatura wird durch eine kleine Achtelnote mit einem schräg durchgestrichenen Hals angezeigt.

Die Acciaccatura wird sehr schnell gespielt und an die nächste Note „gequetscht".

Appoggiatura (vom italienischen Wort „appoggiare": lehnen, anlehnen).
Die Appoggiatura wird ebenfalls durch eine kleine Achtelnote angezeigt, allerdings ohne den schräg durchgestrichenen Hals.

Die Appoggiatura erhält gewöhnlich die Hälfte des Notenwertes der folgenden Note.

Daher wird

wie folgt gespielt

und

folgendermaßen:

Turn

The turn is an ornament which decorates a particular note: the shape is up above the note, down below the note then returning to the original note.

Notated

and played

Notated

and played

Mordent (from the Italian *mòrdere*, meaning to 'bite').

1. The **upper mordent**

is notated

and played

Play the original note itself, the note above and return to the original note, all as quickly as possible.

2. The **lower mordent**

is notated

and played

Play the original note itself, the note below and return to the original note, all as quickly as possible.

Trill

The trill alternates rapidly several times between the written note and the note above.

Whole-tone scale

This is a scale made up entirely of notes a whole-tone apart. There are only two.

Gruppetto

Le *gruppetto* est un ornement qui enjolive une note particulière par un motif qui part de la note supérieure, descend jusqu'à la note inférieure et rejoint la note réelle :

Notation :

Exécution :

Notation :

Exécution :

Mordant (de l'italien *mordere*, mordre).

1. Le **mordant supérieur**

se note :

et se joue :

Jouez le plus vite possible la note réelle, la note supérieure puis la note réelle.

2. Le **mordant inférieur**

se note :

et se joue :

Jouez le plus vite possible la note réelle, la note inférieure puis la note réelle.

Trille

Le trille fait alterner plusieurs fois rapidement la note réelle et la note supérieure.

Gamme par tons

Cette échelle est constituée exclusivement de degrés séparés d'un ton entier. Il n'en existe que deux :

Doppelschlag

Der Doppelschlag ist eine Verzierung, bei der eine bestimmte Note umspielt wird, zuerst mit der oberen Nebennote und dann mit der unteren Nebennote, um schließlich zur Hauptnote zurückzukehren.

Notation:

Spielweise:

Notation:

Spielweise:

Mordent (vom italienischen Wort „mordere": beißen).

1. Der **Pralltriller**

wird wie folgt notiert:

und so gespielt:

Spiele zuerst die Hauptnote, dann die obere Nebennote, und kehre so schnell wie möglich zur Hauptnote zurück.

2. Der **Mordent**

wird wie folgt notiert:

und so gespielt:

Spiele zuerst die Hauptnote, dann die untere Nebennote, und kehre so schnell wie möglich zur Hauptnote zurück.

Triller

Der Triller besteht aus mehreren schnellen Wechseln zwischen einer Note und ihrer oberen Nebennote.

Ganztonleiter

Diese Tonleiter besteht ausschließlich aus Tönen in Ganztonschritten. Es gibt nur zwei Ganztonleitern.

Section 4 – Introducing D♭ major and B major; 5/4, 5/8 and 7/8 time; ornaments

Section 4 – Introduction des tonalités de *ré*♭ majeur et de *si* majeur ; mesures à 5/4, 5/8 et 7/8 ; ornements

Teil 4 – Einführung der Tonarten Des-Dur und H-Dur; Der 5/4-, 5/8- und 7/8-Takt; Verzierungen

86. Risoluto

87. Moderato

88. Ritmico

89.

Dorian mode.   Mode dorien.   Dorisch.

90.

91.

92.

93.

94.

95.

96.

Atonal.   Atonale.   Atonal.

97.

60

Whole tone.   Ton entier.   Auf eine Ganztonleiter aufbauend.

Ornaments.   Ornements.   Verzierungen.

62

105.

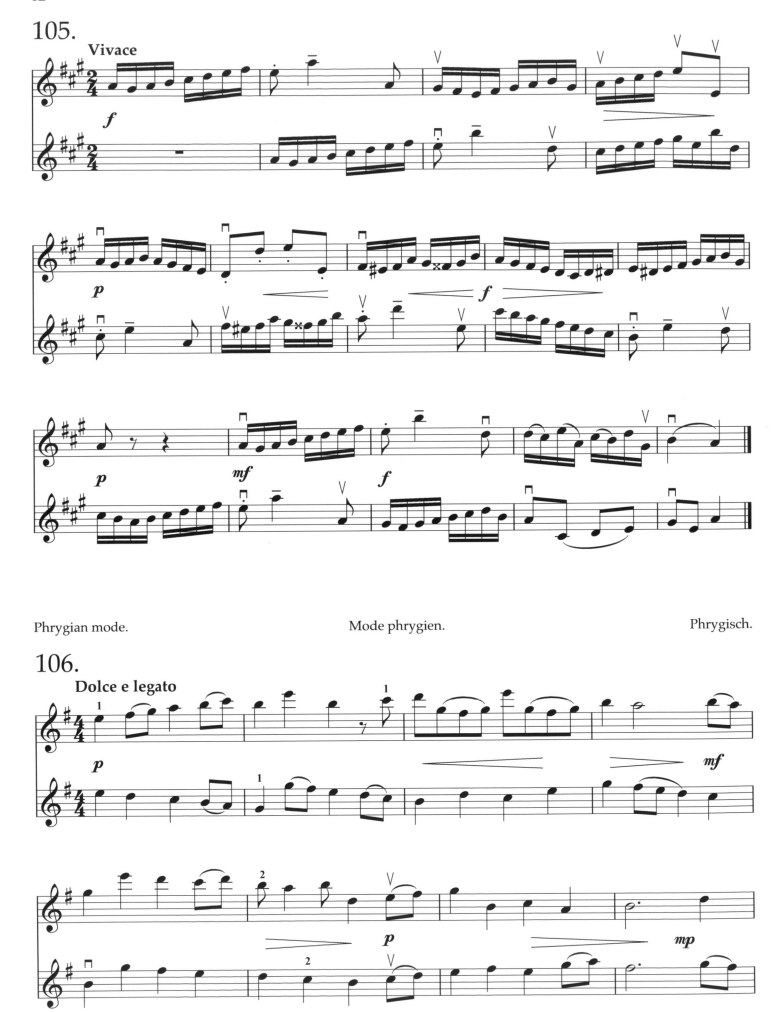

Phrygian mode.   Mode phrygien.   Phrygisch.

106.

107.

108.

Con moto

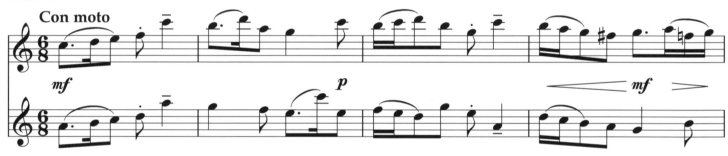

109.

Con moto

110.

Doloroso

111.

112.

113.

114.

69

115.

Doloroso

116.

117.

Molto adagio e mesto

Section 5 – Jigs, reels, time changes, various styles and tonalities

Section 5 – Gigues, *reels*, changements de mesure, tonalités et styles divers

Teil 5 – Jigs, Reels, Taktwechsel, verschiedene Stile und Tonarten

Pentatonic scale (from the Greek 'pente' – five)
The pentatonic scale consists of just five musical notes, omitting all the semitones.
Found when using the black notes on the piano, the pentatonic scale is commonly heard in British folk music and in folk music throughout the world.

Modes
Dating back to ancient Greek times, musical notes were arranged into modes. Each mode has a distinct sound and character. Over the centuries the modes changed and developed, and eventually two of them – the Ionian and the Aeolian – became what we now know as the major and minor scales. We can still hear modes in music that is performed today, in particular in plainsong (the music of the medieval Church) and in the folk music of many countries. Much of today's jazz is based on modes and players learn to use them in their improvisations.

Chromatic patterns
A number of the pieces in this section contain patterns (bits of scales that ascend or descend in semitones). Beware though: sometimes what looks like a portion of a chromatic scale may contain a mixture of movement by tones and semitones.

Gamme pentatonique (du grec, *pente*, cinq)
La gamme pentatonique est constituée de seulement cinq notes, n'incluant pas les demi-tons.
Cette gamme, qui correspond à l'échelle formée par les touches noires du piano, est très présente dans les musiques traditionnelles.

Modes
Du temps de l'antiquité grecque, les notes étaient ordonnées selon des modes qui possédaient leur sonorité et leur caractère propres. Au cours des siècles, les modes se sont modifiés et ont évolué jusqu'à ce que deux d'entre eux – le mode ionien et le mode éolien – nous soient connus comme le mode majeur et le mode mineur. Les modes sont toujours utilisés dans quelques types de musiques comme le plainchant et la musique traditionnelle de certaines régions. La musique de jazz actuelle fait largement appel aux modes et les interprètes apprennent à les utiliser dans leurs improvisations.

Chromatismes
Un certain nombre de pièces de ce volume contiennent des motifs chromatiques (fragments de gammes ascendant ou descendant par demi-tons). Attention, cependant : certains passages ressemblant à des chromatismes peuvent être constitués d'un mélange de tons et de demi-tons.

Pentatonische Tonleiter (vom griechischen Wort „pente": fünf)
Die pentatonische Tonleiter umfasst nur fünf Noten und lässt alle Halbtöne aus.
Auf dem Klavier ist sie leicht zu finden, wenn man nur die schwarzen Tasten verwendet. Die pentatonische Tonleiter wird häufig in der britischen Volksmusik verwendet, aber auch in der Volksmusik der ganzen Welt.

Modi
In der griechischen Musiktheorie wurden die Töne in Modi eingeteilt. Jedes Modus hatte einen bestimmten Klang und Charakter. Im Laufe der Jahrhunderte haben sich die Modi verändert und weiterentwickelt. Zwei von ihnen – der ionische und der äolische Modus – sind zu dem geworden, was wir heute als Dur und Moll bezeichnen. Auch in der heute noch gespielten Musik hören wir verschiedene Modi, besonders in den gregorianischen Chorälen (mittelalterliche Kirchenmusik) und in der Volksmusik vieler Länder. Die meiste Jazzmusik basiert ebenfalls auf Modi; die Musiker lernen, diese bei ihren Improvisationen zu verwenden.

Chromatische Tonfolgen
Etliche Stücke in diesem Kapitel enthalten chromatische Tonfolgen (Teile von Tonleitern, die in Halbtönen auf- oder absteigen). Nimm dich jedoch in Acht: Was manchmal wie ein Teil einer chromatischen Tonleiter aussieht, kann auch eine Mischung aus Ganztönen und Halbtönen sein.

Section 5 – Jigs, reels, time changes, various styles and tonalities

Section 5 – Gigues, *reels*, changements de mesure, tonalités et styles divers

Teil 5 – Jigs, Reels, Taktwechsel, verschiedene Stile und Tonarten

118.

Allegro non troppo

119.

Vivo

120.

121.

122.

Vivace

123.

Vigoroso

124.

Moderato

125. Giocoso

126. Andantino

127. Mazurka

128.

Deciso

129.

Ritmico spiritoso

poco a poco cresc.

rall.

Pentatonic.   Pentatonique.   Pentatonisch.

130.

Moderato

mf legato e espress.

rall. e dim.

78

Dorian mode.　　　　　　　　　　Mode dorien.　　　　　　　　　　Dorisch.

131.

Lydian mode.　　　　　　　　　　Mode lydien.　　　　　　　　　　Lydisch.

132.

Phrygian mode.　　　　　　　　　　Mode phrygien.　　　　　　　　　　Phrygisch.

133.

Whole tone.   Ton entier.   Auf eine Ganztonleiter aufbauend.

134.

Chromatic patterns.   Chromatisme.   Chromatische Muster.

135.

136.

137.

138.

139.

Andante espressivo

140.

Poco adagio

cantabile

141.

142.

Vivace

143.

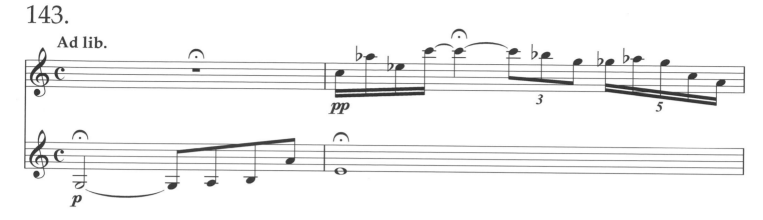

144.

145.

146.

Moderato con rubato

147.

With a slow, bluesy swing ♩ = c.76

148.

149.

Glossary
Glossaire
Glossar

Note performance directions together with their translations used throughout the book so that you have a complete list. Writing them down will help you to remember them.

Inscrivez ici les indications d'exécution utilisées dans ce volume et leur traduction pour en établir une liste complète. Le fait de les noter vous aidera à les retenir.

Schreibe hier alle Vortragszeichen, die im Buch verwendet werden, zusammen mit ihrer Übersetzung auf, so dass du eine vollständige Liste hast. Das Aufschreiben wird dir dabei helfen, sie dir einzuprägen.

Adagio	Slowly	Lent	Langsam